Original title:
Ocean Blue and Coconut Green

Copyright © 2025 Creative Arts Management OÜ
All rights reserved.

Author: Isabella Rosemont
ISBN HARDBACK: 978-1-80581-566-2
ISBN PAPERBACK: 978-1-80581-093-3
ISBN EBOOK: 978-1-80581-566-2

Emerald Isles and Sapphire Skies

On a beach where sand is clingy,
Sunburns make us feel quite swingy.
With drinks adorned with little umbrellas,
We dance like confused, tropical fellas.

The waves shout jokes, splashes are slapstick,
Seagulls dive, they'd call it a trick.
In hammocks strung between two palm trees,
We nap while dreaming of fine cheese.

Sunlit Paths and Oceanic Whispers

Footprints lead us to a coconut shop,
Local monkeys around us hop.
With laughter echoing 'round the bay,
Banter with crabs who wish they could stay.

A beach ball lands right on my nose,
The sun is winning; oh how it glows!
With flip-flops squeaking, we race down the shore,
Tripping on towels, always wanting more.

Lushness by the Water's Edge

In the shade of a giant palm fan,
I saw a crab pulling off a grand plan.
He danced to a tune played by the breeze,
While I giggled, he winked with such ease.

Banana peels turn slapstick to art,
As we trip and stumble, it's all off the chart.
Fish beneath us give an eye roll or two,
They gossip about our beach party crew.

Reverie in the Tropics

In a land alive with vibrant sounds,
Laughter and splashes, joy knows no bounds.
We sip fruity drinks, giggling with glee,
While bugs try to steal the fun from our spree.

The sun sets low, painting skies of pink,
We dance and giggle, barely have time to think.
Under the stars, we make silly bets,
On who'll lose their flip-flops, oh what a sketch!

Melodies of the Sea and Palm

Seagulls laugh on sandy shores,
While crabs dance like they've lost their scores.
Waves tickle toes with a splashing hype,
Fish flip flop, they're the slippery type.

Coconuts giggle high in the trees,
Tickling breezes whisper with ease.
Suntan lotion's a slippery mate,
Making beach strolls a slippery fate.

In the Shade of Aquatic Blues

Under the palm, a funny sight,
Flip-flops hurling, what a flight!
Sunscreen smeared on nose and chin,
With laughter and juice, let the fun begin!

Fish wear sunglasses, who needs a hat?
A dolphin juggles shells, how about that?
Mermaids gossip, giggle, and pout,
While turtles play cards, there's no doubt!

Tidal Dance of Leafy Embrace

The tides do a jig, oh what a spree,
As seaweed twirls like a dancer bold and free.
Shells play maracas, rhythm so bright,
Even the foam joins in the delight.

Limes roll away, a citrus race,
While coconuts wobble, slow in their pace.
Palm fronds sway with a wink and a grin,
Throwing shade at crabs who just can't win!

Echoes of Marine Grace and Rainforest

Bubbles burst in a laughing sound,
As fish chase each other round and round.
Jellyfish wiggle in a silly way,
While dolphins leap, come join the play!

Rainforests chuckle, wearing their crowns,
Mixing with ocean in giggles and frowns.
Mosquitoes dance, a buzzing serenade,
As laughter floats in this verdant parade.

Isle of Enchantment

On this isle, where breezes tease,
Coconuts dance with the swaying trees.
Fish in sunglasses swim and play,
Waves laugh loudly, chasing the day.

Seagulls wear hats, ruffled and bright,
Pelicans juggle with all their might.
Surfboards glide like they've got a plan,
While crabs hold a race, and there's no man.

Bananas in boats float side to side,
With giggles galore, they won't let slide.
Salty breezes tickle your nose,
Making friends with the wiggly toes.

In this land where giggles bloom,
A sea of fun, dispelling gloom.
So grab a drink, sit back and smile,
Join the joy, stay for a while.

Floating through Green-tinted Dreams

In a jungle of laughter, monkeys swing,
With coconuts as their bling-bling thing.
Splashing the water, they take a dive,
Cracking up jokes, keeping fun alive.

Bamboo rafts float, in crazy lines,
While turtles boast about their times.
Colorful fish make a splashy scene,
Dressed in suits that look quite obscene.

Palm trees gossip in huddled groups,
Sharing tales of adventurous loops.
A parrot squawks, "Is that a whale?"
He's just confused; it's a wiggly snail.

Underwater tea parties make a wave,
With sardines serving, looking quite brave.
Cupcakes bob in the bubbly dance,
What a riot of colors, oh what a chance!

Land Where Colors Whisper

In a realm where hues enjoy a spree,
A green frog sings by the bouncy sea.
With keys in his pocket and socks on his feet,
He croaks out rhythms, oh so neat!

The sun wears shades, looking so cool,
While flip-flops strut, breaking every rule.
A shrimp in a tux brings laughter around,
As he tap-dances on the sandy ground.

Chameleons play hide-and-seek all day,
Wearing wacky colors on their display.
Laughter erupts from the sandy shore,
As waves crash in, begging for more.

Join in the fun, let your worries float,
In this land where colors hardly bloat.
Just smiles and giggles, an endless seam,
Welcome to your wildest dream!

Fronds and Foam in Harmonious Grace

The waves giggle and splash a tune,
While palm leaves dance beneath the moon.
A crab in a bow tie takes the stage,
With a flip and a dip, he's quite the sage.

Seagulls squawk in a silly parade,
While sandcastles melt, a beach escapade.
The sun wears shades, and so does the sand,
Laughing as they join this merry band.

Echoes of a Coastal Dream

A fish in a tuxedo swims with flair,
While dolphins hoopla through salty air.
A starfish holds a mic and sings,
While sea turtles dance on silky strings.

The breeze tells jokes, the shells all chuckle,
As beach balls bounce and tumble with puddles.
Crabs wearing hats join in the fun,
In this land where silly never is done.

Celestial Greens of the Daybreak

The morning laughs with citrus bright,
While kites in the sky take a flight.
A parrot mimics a silly tune,
While coconuts sway and croon.

Lizards play tag on vibrant beams,
Sipping sunshine and tasty creams.
The day begins with bubbling glee,
As nature grins, wild and free.

Embracing Nature's Palette

The colors clash in a joyful mess,
As fruits in baskets play dress to impress.
The waves go 'whoosh' while they frolic around,
With seaweed hats and laughter abound.

A beach ball bounces on a sunny throne,
While flip-flops tango and drift alone.
Nature's whimsy paints the day,
In hues of fun where silliness sways.

Tropical Hues and Sunlit Views

The sun wore shades, a silly sight,
While crabs danced around, feeling quite light.
Bright drinks in hand, on a float we lay,
Laughing at clouds that drifted away.

The breeze played tricks, like a playful tease,
Tickling our noses, rustling the trees.
With laughter as loud as the waves in a roar,
We found our fun on that sandy shore.

Beneath a Canopy of Stars

Stars twinkled down, like eyes in the night,
As we chased fireflies, what a delight!
The moon wore a crown of coconut leaves,
Tickling our feet, with secrets it weaves.

Laughter echoed, a melody bright,
As crickets joined in, what a funny sight!
We dubbed the night 'a confetti spree',
With dreams tangled up like a wild jubilee.

Dreaming under a Lush Sky

Napping on hammocks, a swing and a sway,
Dreams of big fish, and a playful ray.
A parrot squawked, sharing secrets untold,
While we drizzled jelly on pancakes of gold.

The sky laughed in colors, a doodle of glee,
With clouds that did flips, oh, how wild we'd be!
We munched on sweet fruits, giggling away,
In this paradise, forever we'd stay.

A Canvas of Mist and Palm

Morning broke out with a giggling sun,
We painted our hopes, oh what funny fun!
With brushes of waves and strokes of lime,
Each splash of color felt truly sublime.

But oh! The paint splattered, a rainbow mess,
We laughed and we danced in our soggy dress.
The palm trees swayed to our silly tune,
As we waved goodnight to the silly moon.

Unveiling Nature's Brushstrokes

Waves crash like a clumsy dance,
Shells giggle in a sandy trance.
Seagulls squawk a cheeky tune,
While crabs play hide and seek by the dune.

Laughter bubbles in salty breeze,
As fish put on their show with ease.
A sunbeam winks, oh what a sight,
Nature's palette brings pure delight!

Captured by Immersive Hues

In a hammock, sipping drinks so bright,
I toast to colors of pure delight.
Bees make art in the clover patch,
While my flip-flops try to find a match.

Coconut hats upon our heads,
Sunshine dances on hammock beds.
Laughter floats like clouds up high,
As time drifts slowly, oh my, oh my!

Driftwood Dreams in Canopy Light

Driftwood sculptures, what a sight,
Trees wearing costumes that feel just right.
Lizards prance with swagger and flair,
While I try not to lose my hair.

Sunlight splashes through leafy skies,
As branches whisper their playful lies.
Nature sings a lively tune,
While I sneak snacks like a raccoon!

Breathing Sunkissed Air

Sandy toes and sunburned nose,
Laughter echoes where the wind blows.
My drink's a rainbow, oh so sweet,
As the beach towels perform a feat.

Waves tickle my feet with all their might,
While dolphins dance with pure delight.
Underneath a sun so bright,
We find joy in every bite!

Sailing Through Different Shades

On a boat made of dreams, we paddled all day,
With seagulls as lifeguards, so goofy and gay.
The waves whispered jokes, the sun wore a grin,
And fish jumped aboard to join in the spin.

We sailed on a rainbow, just us and the breeze,
Chasing fins and tales, and napping on knees.
A clam threw a party, we danced with a crab,
While the turtles all laughed at our silly flab.

Our sails flapped like flags with a humorous twist,
As dolphins played tag, we couldn't resist.
With laughter and splashes, we conquered the tide,
In a friendship so silly, we took it in stride.

Splashes of Spirit

In a cove made of giggles, we splashed in a line,
With buckets of coconut, that tasted divine.
We dodged all the waves like they were on strike,
While the crabs at the shore were ready to hike.

A pelican swooped, aimed right for my hat,
I dodged like a ninja, oh imagine that!
The laughter erupted, the sun shone so bright,
As we played hide and seek with the rays of daylight.

The sand tickled toes with its warm, silly charm,
As we built up a fortress, a castle from palm.
With every new splash, a giggle did rise,
These moments of joy, the ultimate prize.

A Paradise Awaits

With piña coladas served in shells made for two,
We lounged in the sun, not a care in our view.
The hammock was swinging, a coconuts' dream,
Where laughter and sunlight wove a golden seam.

The parrots were gossiping, squawking their news,
About some funny tourists in mismatched shoes.
We joined in the chatter, while sipping our drink,
And they cheered when I slipped, fell right in the sink!

The breeze sang a tune, a delightful refrain,
As waves played the drums, a tropical gain.
In a paradise painted with giggles and cheer,
We danced with the sunset, oh what a career!

Tangled between Fisherman and Forest

Beneath leafy giants where the fishermen dream,
We tangled our lines with a comical theme.
A fish swung a byline, "Can I join the show?"
And laughter erupted like a curious flow.

With bait in our pockets and joy in our hearts,
We cast off our worries, just silly old arts.
The forest was booming with chatter and cheer,
As we fished for some fun, maybe ales, maybe beer.

Each tug on the line brought a new silly tale,
While the squirrels cheered on our deep-sea sail.
In a world made of chuckles, we snagged a big catch,
A festival of laughter, oh what a great match!

Breeze-Kissed Indigo and Leafy Light

The waves make funny faces, oh so wide,
As shells argue over who has the best tide.
Seagulls dance like they're on a wild spree,
While crabs put on shows, just for you and me.

With drinks in hand, we sip the cool breeze,
Sunburned noses, trying to dodge the bees.
Flip-flops flop as we race to the shore,
Laughter erupts, who could ask for more?

A fish with a grin darts past with a wink,
Underwater parties make dolphins rethink.
Their belly-flops leave us rolling in glee,
A fishy fiesta as grand as can be!

So here we sit, with sand on our toes,
In this silly paradise, anything goes.
The sun dips low, and we cheer out loud,
For the joy of the waves, we're forever proud.

Caribbean Serenade in Teal and Jade

A parrot sings tunes that tickle the ear,
While coconut smoothies bring holiday cheer.
Sunburned tourists in hats way too bright,
Try dancing the limbo, what a hilarious sight!

The hammock sways, a nap is in sight,
But mosquitoes have staged a daring night fight.
With swats and giggles, we battle the swarm,
In our tropical fortress, it's quite the charm!

A sandcastle towers, with flags made of leaves,
While jet skis zoom like mischievous thieves.
The crabs take a tour, it's quite the parade,
With sandy confetti, no plans need to fade!

So let's raise a glass to this wacky scene,
Where dolphins surf and the scenery's green.
With laughter and joy, we'll dance till the night,
In this paradise, everything feels just right!

Celestial Waters and Tropical Traces

Stars twinkle brightly above a broad sea,
While fish form a band, all singing in glee.
A curious turtle knocks at our door,
With a wink and a nod, he asks for some more!

Inflatable flamingos float in a line,
They're having a race, and they think they're divine.
We cheer and we laugh as they bob in the tide,
What a grand struggle—every bird's a 'slide'!

Sandy footprints create silly maps,
As we dodge the crabs and their funny little naps.
The tide rolls in with a rumble and splash,
While beach balls bounce with an energetic crash!

So let's celebrate with a joyous shout,
For this whimsical trip, we can't live without.
With friends by our side and laughter to spare,
In this vibrant land, fun hangs in the air!

The Dance of Aquatic Limes

A lime rolls down, what a comical sight,
It bounces and spins, oh what pure delight!
Bikinis and board shorts are dancing around,
With beach tunes blasting, joy knows no bound!

Crabs in a conga line sway to the tune,
Their tiny legs tapping like stars in June.
Seashells and sand join this fabulous show,
As the sun takes a bow, putting on a glow.

A game of beach frisbee turns into a chase,
As we chase our hats in this frolicsome race.
With splashes and laughter, we're free as the breeze,
In this zany limeland, we do as we please!

So grab your limeade, and join the parade,
The fun never stops when good vibes are made.
In this tropical haven with friends oh so prime,
We'll dance through the waves, one wacky lime-time!

Colors of Paradise

In a world where fish wear shoes,
And palm trees share their views,
The waves do samba, quite a sight,
As crabs prove they can dance all night.

A parrot's laugh, a monkey's grin,
Coconut balls are where they spin,
The sun shines down with a playful glare,
While seagulls gossip without a care.

Celestial Waters and Fertile Greens

Under skies of twisty sherbet,
The turtles race with quite a threat,
While mermaids swap their tales for jokes,
And dolphins join in, cracking pokes.

The grasshoppers wear cool sun hats,
While squids serve drinks to chatty chaps,
With every wave that tickles toes,
The ocean's sense of humor grows.

When Coral Meets Canopy

In jungles where the parrots squawk,
The fish all gossip as they walk,
Beneath the canopy's green embrace,
There's laughter all around this place.

A sloth shares puns with a high-flying kite,
While jellyfish share jokes about fright,
The harmony sings, a comical tune,
As trees and reefs dance beneath the moon.

Glimmering Wishes in the Boughs

In vibrant glades where laughter flows,
And flip-flops stomp on sandy toes,
The dreams of crabs take flight at night,
As twinkling stars join in the light.

Coconuts roll while seagulls cheer,
As palm trees sway with lively cheer,
In this wonderland, the jests abound,
Where green and blue wear smiles profound.

Underneath a Tropic Tale

Beneath the palms, a crab does dance,
With tiny legs, he takes a chance.
He trips on shells, falls on his back,
The jungle giggles, echoes the crack.

A parrot talks, with such great flair,
Telling secrets of the salty air.
"Don't ask the fish! They're quite a bore!"
The parrot squawks, and we all roar.

The sun is bright, the drinks are cool,
Yet someone's sliding into the pool.
With splash and bash, the laughter flies,
Like crabs in shorts, we say our goodbyes.

Connecting Depths and Heights

A dolphin dives, then pops for a joke,
Says he's the king of seaweed smoke.
A seagull laughs, a squid rolls his eye,
While jellyfish wait, simply to fly.

Turtles in shades take a leisurely stroll,
One claims he's the coolest of all in the shoal.
With stories so wild, they draw quite a crowd,
While fish in the back seem quiet and proud.

The sun sets low, it's time for a feast,
The crabs bring snacks, a ridiculous beast!
They dance and they twirl, with bread rolls in tow,
And all through the night, the fun seems to grow.

Chasing Shadows across the Shore

Footprints in sand, but which way to go?
We follow the seagull, he seems in the know.
But he takes a detour, mistaken in flight,
Now we're lost under the moon's gentle light.

We find a lost flip-flop, it's missing its pair,
A party for soles with no one to spare!
The wind starts to play, with laughter ablaze,
As shadows conspire in a comical maze.

A sunset of colors, faceplants galore,
As tourists collide and fall down the shore.
Head over heels, we each take a turn,
In this beachy circus, there's always to learn.

Tides of Serenity

A scoop of sunshine, a sprinkle of salt,
With toppings of laughter, and noihng feels small.
The waves whisper secrets, the sands tickle toes,
As crabs run for cover in their crustacean clothes.

The surfboards are ready, but who's in a rush?
We'll paddle on in, in a colorful hush.
With splashes and giggles, we ride the great tides,
And wipeouts galore keep our humor alive.

The tide is our friend, it pulls us along,
As the breeze playfully sings us a song.
So here's to the fun, the mess and the cheer,
With each wave, we dance, let go of our fear!

Turquoise Horizons and Evergreens

Under skies of playful hues,
Palm trees sway and dance with views.
Seagulls squawk, a feathery crowd,
While beachgoers laugh, oh so loud.

Flip-flops slapping on warm sand,
Ice cream melting, oh so bland.
A crab in a hat, struts his stuff,
Claiming beach space, oh how tough!

Laughter bounces on the breeze,
As clumsy surfers attempt to seize.
Wave upon wave, they tumble and roll,
Chasing the sunset, seeking their goal.

With each sip of coconut delight,
Silly grins and pure delight.
The horizon beckons, bright and wide,
Join us here, let joy abide!

Silhouettes of Nautical Greenery

Pineapple hats on heads so bold,
Chasing shadows, stories told.
Flying fish, a jolly tease,
Gliding by with such great ease.

Sandcastles rise, under sun's glow,
With moats filled with giggles, watch them flow.
Fishermen's tales, slightly askew,
Catch of the day? Just a shoe!

Mermaids waving from behind rocks,
Toasting with coconuts, not clocks.
Sandy feet and silly games,
Rhythms of laughter, no one to blame.

Under stars, the beach does gleam,
With soggy snacks, they all scream.
As the moon laughs, shining above,
We dance together, in pure love!

Aquatic Symphony beneath Canopy

Bubbles rise in joyful bursts,
Floating by, the silly firsts.
Turtles wearing floral shirts,
Spinning tales of summer flirts.

Corals laugh with colors bright,
As rays of sun feel just right.
Crayons on the shore create,
Drawings of a fish named Nate.

Tropical birds, a loud parade,
Singing tunes while folks invade.
Kites soaring high, trailing glee,
Watch your sandwich, here comes a bee!

Dance with the sand, twist and twirl,
Laughter wraps around each whirl.
Under the canopy of dreams so wide,
Join the fun, step inside!

Sailors of the Verdant Isle

Sailor hats and coconut drinks,
Finding treasure, what fun it thinks.
A parrot squawks secrets and lies,
While socks have a war 'gainst salty tides.

Glimmering waves, a frothy plot,
Chasing fish, why not give it a shot?
In the distance, laughter sounds,
As a crab solves riddles, wearing crowns.

Captain's log, a series of blunders,
Navigating laughter, amidst the wonders.
With dedicated maps made of sand,
The treasure's here, just as planned!

Anchors away with buddy ships,
While rainbows dance on sassy lips.
With smiles and jokes that never cease,
On this journey, we find our peace!

Seafoam Dreams entwined with Foliage

The waves whisper secrets to the sand,
Coconuts chuckle, they've got a band.
Palms sway like dancers in a wild breeze,
While crabs wear sunglasses, feeling at ease.

A fish with a tie swims by with glee,
He's got a date with a starfish, you see.
The seaweed winks, a playful tease,
Jellyfish giggle, drifting with ease.

Seagulls trade jokes while soaring high,
One stole a flip-flop! What a sly guy!
Saltwater laughter fills the warm air,
As flip-flops and dreams are tossed everywhere.

In a coconut shell, a party begins,
With little shrimp sipping on their fins.
Join the fun, let your worries be few,
In this leafy haven where joy's overdue.

Where the Sun Meets the Sea

Under the sun's warm, golden beam,
The clams have a contest for the best cream.
Surfers are tumbling, looking quite frantic,
While mermaids are giggling at their antics.

Sandcastles sprout like mushrooms in rain,
With a moat that protects from silly disdain.
A crab in a crown plots to take over,
While a turtle just shrugs, calling it a dover.

As the sun dips low, cocktails are nifty,
With umbrellas bright, the vibe turns shifty.
Fish wearing bowties join in the fun,
Trying to dance in the sky, just to stun.

The horizon blushes, painting great sights,
While dolphins burst forth in spontaneous flights.
Everyone chuckles, losing track of time,
In a whirl of laughter, life's simply sublime.

The Dance of Tropical Tides

The waves jump higher, they're ready to groove,
Turtles are busting a move, making a prove.
Coconuts roll along, trying to skate,
While fish in bowties are running quite late.

As the moon rises, the shells start to hum,
The starfish tap dance, making quite the drum.
Crabs do the limbo, all in a row,
While seahorses sway, putting on a show.

Under the stars, the night feels alive,
With shrimp spinning tales like they've just arrived.
A clam with a trumpet plays jazzy tunes,
Inviting the gulls for a dance under moons.

With laughter and music, the night's in full swing,
Even the dolphins are learning to sing.
So, join in the revels, dance without care,
In this quirky kingdom where joy fills the air.

Secrets Cradled in the Dunes

In the soft dunes, secrets are hiding,
With crabs playing poker, none are abiding.
Turtles take naps on the sandy warm beds,
While gulls share tall tales about their feast spreads.

Sandy footprints lead to a treasure of laughs,
Where octopuses argue over silly gaffs.
Seashells gossip, their whispers are sweet,
While a lizard in flips flops steals the big beat.

A wave with a wig crashes down with flair,
Tickling the toes of those wandering there.
Seagulls squawk loudly, stealing the scene,
While the beachcombers dance with the pickled marine.

In the gathering twilight, the light starts to fade,
And laughter echoes where joys never trade.
So, here in the dunes, let's keep these old jokes,
In the heart of the coast where silliness pokes.

Turquoise Echoes

A fish named Fred wore a big red hat,
He danced with crabs on a floating mat.
Seagulls laughed as they swooped low,
While turtles watched the most ridiculous show.

The jellyfish twirled in shiny bling,
While whales tried hard to join in the swing.
With splashes and giggles, they spun around,
Creating a party beneath the sound.

Bubbles burst with tales of silly sights,
As starfish joined in with their dazzling lights.
The rhythm of waves brought laughter anew,
In waters where giggles and glimmers grew.

So come along, hear the silly cheer,
With fishy friends, there's nothing to fear.
In this splashy place of bright colors and gleams,
Life's all about fun, or so it seems!

Tropical Tranquility

In a hammock swinging, a parrot sang,
While a coconut fell with a resounding clang.
Monkeys laughed, stealing bananas away,
And lizards lounged, enjoying the play.

A crab in shades tried to impress,
But stumbled back, causing a mess.
Fish waved around in bubble-blown cheer,
Saying, "Life's a beach—bring on the beer!"

Pineapples grin on the sandy shore,
While pesky bugs gather to explore.
The sunsets flash, a sky painted bright,
Making it hard to tell day from night.

All creatures join as the moon climbs high,
With giggles and howlers echoing the sky.
In this lively paradise, life's all about glee,
With every moment as wild as can be!

Melodies of Coral Reefs

Coral dancers in gowns made of lace,
Spin and twirl in their underwater space.
Crabs play the drums with a clappy shell,
As fish throw confetti, oh what a swell!

A clownfish jokes with no sense of fear,
Telling tales that all critters could hear.
A dolphin joins in with flips and a dive,
Making this reef a party alive!

Starfish grin with their five-pointed charm,
While anemones sway like they're on a farm.
The bubbles that rise hold laughter in tow,
In this watery world where silliness flows.

So gather around, here's where we thrive,
With fins, flops, and laughter—we're all alive!
In the heart of the reef, let good times renew,
Celebrating this joy in colorful hues!

A Symphony of Waves and Leaves

The palm trees sway to the rhythm of cheer,
With a toucan squawking, loud and clear.
Crickets chirp in a melodious tune,
While sandcastles melt by the light of the moon.

Sea turtles strut, all dressed up for the day,
While jellybeans float, come join the fray.
With a wink to the sun and a nod to the breeze,
Life's a grand concert of laughter and ease.

The waves crash down with a playful roar,
As kids on the beach giggle and explore.
Shells play the trumpets, each one a surprise,
Creating a symphony under bright skies.

At dusk, the stars wink, sharing their jest,
While the moon giggles, a playful guest.
So dance with the waves, let your spirit run free,
In this whimsical place, just you and the sea!

Verdant Breezes and Seafoam Dreams

In a hammock tied to a tiny tree,
I found a coconut sipping tea.
A gull asked for a taste, I said, "No way!"
He squawked and flew off, thinking of the fray.

The waves giggle as they kiss the shore,
Tickling my toes, asking for more.
I laughed so hard, I spilled my drink,
Now the crabs are planning, what do you think?

Mermaids blush as they watch me fall,
While a dolphin emits a joyful call.
A fish, in a tux, looks quite impressed,
But all I can do is awkwardly rest.

So I sing with the breeze and dance with the tide,
With each whispered secret, I take in my stride.
A party under the stars, a splash and a cheer,
Would you join this hullabaloo? Please, don't fear!

Beyond the Cove of Swaying Palms

A crab in sunglasses struts down the sand,
Claiming his patch, it's all quite grand.
But here come the waves, splash-bang in line,
He's left with a shell, oh how divine!

Palm fronds are swaying, lost in delight,
The breeze whispers secrets all through the night.
A parrot swings by with a wink and a squawk,
He asks for a piña colada, let's rock!

But oh! What's that—a painted seashell?
It's actually a crab in a rave, can you tell?
With beats from the tide and groovy moves,
We all join together, finding the grooves.

Now I'm the DJ, with a shell for my mic,
Jellyfish jelly in a bowl, what a sight!
A conch starts to whistle, and laughter erupts,
With a flip and a splash, fun is construct!

The Allure of Aqua and Leafy Veil

The sun wears shades, a hat quite wide,
As fish blow bubbles, they all take pride.
Caught in a net of comic slapstick,
Octopus juggling, what a neat trick!

The seaweed waves like it's on a call,
As friends in flip-flops trip, oh what a fall!
Laughter erupts, even turtles join in,
With a snort and a giggle, they all wear a grin.

Seashells are singing their own little song,
Who knew they could do that all along?
With twirls and splashes, we dance in delight,
In this wacky wonder, we party all night.

So here's to the laughter, the splash and the glee,
With every flip-flop, we're wild and carefree.
The sun sets in colors of pink and gold,
In this whimsical paradise, where stories unfold!

Enchanted Shores of Teal and Green

A dolphin flipped by, with a wink and grin,
He claimed he could dance, let the fun begin!
With seaweed confetti floating around,
The beach became lively, oh what a sound!

A sunburnt seagull stole someone's fries,
While starfish giggled, using surprise eyes.
Lemonade splashed, a tropical toast,
To sea critters plotting, who loves the most?

Turtles in shades break-dancing by,
While crabs form a band, oh my, oh my!
With each splat and crash of waves on the shore,
We're caught in a whirlwind, laughter galore!

So join the parade, don't shy away,
With goofy antics, let's dance and play.
In this silly kingdom where good times abound,
Every wave tells a joke, let's gather around!

Tropical Echoes Beneath Sky and Leaf

Underneath the palm's embrace,
Silly crabs do a wacky race.
Seagulls laugh as they swoop down,
Wearing shells like a party crown.

Bouncing waves tickle your toes,
While a turtle strikes a pose.
Coconuts dance on the shore,
One rolls away; oh, what a chore!

Fruits swing from the leafy heights,
While monkeys plan their silly flights.
Laughter bubbles in the breeze,
Tickling noses like soft tease.

Time for fun beneath the sun,
Pop those drinks, let's all run!
Life's a game, let's play it well,
With sandy toes, we cast a spell.

Sapphire Currents and Jungle Shadows

Waves are jumping, whales are singing,
While a parrot mocks what we're bringing.
Underwater, fish throw a bash,
With disco lights and a thrilling splash.

Trees are shaking with a giggle,
Monkeys swing with a wild wiggle.
Crabs offer drinks, served with a grin,
Laughter echoes beneath the din.

Sunflowers try to steal the show,
But they're stuck in the mud, oh no!
Watermelons roll with laughter bold,
Tropical antics never get old.

The breeze drops jokes and holds the key,
To a party where all are free.
So join the fun, take a seat,
With snacks galore, it's quite the treat!

Glistening Waters and Foliage Fire

Streams are shining, a glimmering spree,
While fish charm with their splishy spree.
Each ripple whispers a joke so neat,
Even the crabs can't help but tweet!

Where the shadows dance and sway,
We play hopscotch in the midday ray.
Turtles claim they're the best at chess,
Who knew they'd sport such a wild dress?

The breeze tries to tickle the trees,
Shaking loose coconuts with ease.
While pineapples rock like they're on stage,
We laugh together, freed from our cage.

At sunset, the party gets loud,
With laughter echoing, we're all proud.
Join the fun, and don't you fret,
For the night is young, as a true duet!

The Rhythm of Verdant Waves

The green below sways like a dance,
With surprising moves, come take a chance.
Flamingos flip and let out a cheer,
While a turtle struts in front, oh dear!

Pineapples gossip under the sun,
Claiming coconut jokes—what fun!
While the sun dips low, crabs throw a bash,
Boogie-ing down with a wild flash.

Seashells chime a merry tune,
Disco nights beneath the moon.
Every splash joins in the play,
As glow sticks twirl in a bright ballet.

So, grab a friend and hit the sand,
With jokes and giggles, hand in hand.
In this leafy paradise, nothing's wrong,
Join the laughter; come along!

The Rhythm of Tropical Waves

The surf sings songs of frothy brew,
While crabs take dances on the view.
Seagulls squawk in silly glee,
As dolphins play a game with tea.

Bananas wear sunscreens, so bright,
While waves make all the fish take flight.
A coconut smiles, jokes on his face,
Rolling away with a clumsy grace.

Flip-flops flop like fish on land,
As kids dig castles in the sand.
Tropical drinks with silly straws,
Raise a toast to nature's flaws.

With every wave, a giggle spreads,
As palm trees sway like dancing heads.
A crab with shades, oh what a sight,
Under the sun, feeling just right.

Green Canopy over Azure Depths

Under leaves, the monkey grins,
Stealing snacks while everyone spins.
Mangoes drop with a thud and bounce,
Squirrels argue over where to pounce.

The old turtle takes his time,
Claiming he's the master of rhyme.
While fish in costumes swim around,
In the currents of joy, laughter's found.

A beetle wears a tiny hat,
Thinking he's cool, can you imagine that?
Green vines laugh as they twist and twine,
It's a party for nature – how divine!

With every rustle, the jungle pokes,
Telling jokes in ancient croaks.
Laughing leaves, a breath of cheer,
In this green world, we spread the cheer.

Caribbean Whisperings

A parrot squawks with a flair so grand,
While turtles race on the shimmering sand.
The breeze tells tales of silly quests,
As fish wear hats and do their best.

The sun plays peek-a-boo in the sky,
With clouds that tickle as they float by.
A big old starfish with a bright pink hue,
Swears he once danced with a fish in blue.

Jellyfish jiggle in a wiggly tease,
As the crabs perform in the salty breeze.
Seashells gossip, sharing news,
"Did you hear? The sun just lost its shoes!"

Every splash is a chuckle, a delight,
As kids splash wildly with pure delight.
In this paradise where giggles reign,
Each wave whispers laughter again and again.

Dappled Light on Sandy Shores

Footprints shuffle on the warm appeal,
Where shadows dance and laughter's real.
Beach balls bouncing, oh what a game,
As sunscreen battles with a slippery claim.

A crab in shades, oh what a style,
Pushing its rock with a goofy smile.
Sandcastles crumble, but who really cares?
A playful feud with the ocean's snares.

Kites soar high in a colorful race,
While squished ice cream melts all over the place.
Picnics turn to laughter and crumbs,
As seagulls plot their tricky sums.

The sun dips low, painting the sky,
While all around, the giggles fly.
In every wave, a story appears,
Of sunny days and endless cheers.

Between the Jungle and the Sea

Amidst the trees where monkeys swing,
A coconut falls, what a silly thing!
Splash on a pirate, oh what a sight,
Laughter erupts, from day till night.

Crabs in the sand, they scuttle and race,
Waving their claws, like they're in a chase.
Fish poke their heads, in a playful way,
Calling us all to come out and play.

A toucan giggles, perched high in a tree,
Sipping sweet nectar, oh how carefree!
With each little wave, a tickle and tease,
Life in this paradise, oh such a breeze.

So here's to the fun, from jungle to tide,
In this goofy land, we'll forever abide!
Grab your sunscreen, and let's start the show,
Between the green leaves and the waters that glow.

Surf and Sanctuary

Catch that wave, but don't wipe out!
Beach bunnies giggle, without a doubt.
Sunshine and surf, the perfect pair,
Holding our boards, with wind in our hair.

Seagulls line up for a share of the fries,
One swoops down, what a crafty surprise!
Sand castles crumble, but we don't mind,
With salty hair and a laughter unconfined.

Dolphins perform in a bright ballet,
They jump and they spin, in a cheeky way.
"Hey humans, watch us, we're king of the sea!"
As we crack up, sipping iced teas with glee.

So let's surf the wave of silly delight,
Where every splash brings laughter and light.
With friends at our side, oh what a view,
In this sanctuary, where fun feels brand new.

Kaleidoscope of the Tropics

Colors collide, a wild parade,
Parrots squawk loud, in this sunny glade.
Banana peels slip, and down we go,
Rolling in giggles, with a tropical flow.

The sun's on a mission, to toast us today,
While pineapples chuckle, in their fruity way.
Mangoes are bouncing, like they're at a ball,
Who knew fruit could have such a call?

Cocktails clink loudly, we toast to the sun,
With tiny umbrellas, we're having such fun.
A piña colada takes center stage,
As we dance in the sand, letting joy engage.

So here in the splash, let's laugh a bit more,
With each wave that crashes against the shore.
In this kaleidoscope, all worries flee,
Join the fiesta, just come be free!

The Allure of Island Bliss

Hammocks are swinging, oh what a treat,
Swinging and swaying, it feels so sweet.
A seagull drops chips, what a funny fail,
We laugh with delight at this wacky tale.

Sunshine is shining, on blue jellyfish,
They wiggle and jive, granting our wish.
Flip-flops a-flapping, we take to the shore,
With grins like children, craving for more.

An iguana poses, so cool in the heat,
Sunglasses perched and looking quite neat.
As waves crash around, we burst with glee,
In this paradise, just you wait and see.

So let's toast to laughter, with sand in our toes,
In this blissful place, where fun always grows.
With each silly moment, let's cherish and sing,
For the joy of this island, oh what a fling!

Serene Shores and Lush Vistas

The waves come in with a splashy dance,
While crabs conspire for a sideways prance.
Seagulls gossip about the sun's great flair,
As sunscreen fights the wind with heated care.

Palm trees giggle in the sun's warm light,
Their coconuts bolted down, held tight.
A beach ball wobbles on a curious breeze,
While flip-flops wander, teasing with ease.

Umbrellas flutter like flags of delight,
As sunscreen streaks make everyone quite a sight.
Kids chase sandcastles, dreams in flight,
While adults just nap, pretending it's night.

With laughter and splashes, the hours drift,
As the tide plays tricks, oh what a gift!
Here on this shore where the humor's so fine,
Every sand grain laughs, sipping coconut wine.

The Tranquil Tropics Unfold

In the shade of palms, I munch on a snack,
Fruits fall from trees, just like a joke on the track.
Monkeys swing by, full of cheeky spree,
Stealing my hat, oh how can this be?

Comical crabs don their little red suits,
While fish throw parties in bright, shiny boots.
The sunsets giggle with colors so bold,
As the waves roll in with stories retold.

Laughter erupts with every wave's crash,
As the breeze whispers secrets of a mustache bash.
Look out for surfboards, they jump and they spin,
Taking the plunge, a splash or a win!

With each sandy footprint, we leave behind,
Stories of folly, a laughter designed.
In this paradise, joy's our main goal,
As we wade through the surf, heart and soul whole.

Currents of Grass and Celestial Zephyr.

The grass waves back, as if in a race,
While clouds frown upon our goofy face.
Breezes flit by with a tickle and tease,
As kites dance above, with the greatest of ease.

Sipping cool drinks, we squint at the sun,
As locusts play tunes, oh what quirky fun!
The leaves start to shake, with mischief in tow,
As butterflies tumble, putting on a show.

Kangaroos bounce to the beat of a tune,
While llamas debate under the laughing moon.
Silly grasshoppers leap and they fling,
As we sit back and let the laughter ring.

With giggles and grins, the day fades to night,
Under stars that shimmer, oh what a sight!
In this verdant realm, where merriment beams,
Every creature joins in the dance of our dreams.

Whispers of the Tidal Breeze

Waves play peek-a-boo, hiding with glee,
While foam tickles toes, oh the mystery!
Figs droop with laughter, in the sun's warm hand,
As laughter in spray flutters through the sand.

Dolphins tumble and turn, a cheeky parade,
While jellyfish joke about plans they have laid.
A dog on the shore digs with furious might,
Uncovering treasures by pure, silly light.

Everyone's sun-kissed, from head to the toe,
With ice cream dripping, putting on quite a show.
A seagull swoops down, grabs snacks with a caw,
As the tide pulls back, revealing a flaw.

With chuckles and splashes, we all take a dive,
In this coastal circus, oh how we thrive!
Beneath the sun's grin, we find our sweet fix,
In this whimsical world, filled with tricks and quick flicks.

Salty Kisses and Leafy Embraces

Splashing waves chase my feet,
While palm fronds sway to the beat.
Seagulls squawk with crazy flair,
Chasing shadows in midair.

Coconuts tumble, no time to sip,
As I dodge the fishy flip.
A crab stares with a sideways glance,
While I attempt a beach dance.

Sand forms castles, a royal spree,
With turrets made of seaweed, you see!
In this kingdom, I claim my throne,
But wave crashes, and I'm overthrown!

Laughter echoes down the shore,
Losing flip-flops? Oh, what a chore!
But with a grin, I run along,
The salty air my joyful song.

The Color of Serenity

The sky wears a bright blue bow,
Where thoughts drift like clouds below.
I surf the breeze on a board of dreams,
While ice cream melts and sunlight beams.

Flipping over a floating mat,
I spot a turtle in a hat!
He waves hello with a gentle nod,
I laugh so hard, it feels like a prod.

Seashells giggle beneath my toes,
Like secrets from where the river flows.
A crab doing yoga, quite a scene,
Pose as a lobster, if you know what I mean!

Waves whisper riddles as I drift,
With every splash, my spirits lift.
Who knew the sea had such a flair,
For tickling my funny bone in the air?

Shades of Lagoon and Leaf

Under palm trees, laughter rings,
As monkeys dance and do silly things.
With coconuts rolling off the stand,
I juggle them, not quite as planned.

The fish parade in their shiny suits,
With guffaws from seashells in their boots.
I try to dive, but oh, so slow,
And end up face-first in a row!

Crab races start as the tide rolls in,
One's lost a shoe, oh where's he been?
The seagulls dance, quite the display,
While I attempt to run away!

So let's toast to the skies so bright,
With nothing but giggles as our delight.
The lagoon teems with fun galore,
Jump in feet first, and let's explore!

Verdure against the Seabed

A blanket of green on sandy floor,
Where fish gossip and crabs galore.
I tread lightly, don't want to trip,
On the seaweed's slippery grip!

A shrimp with shades gives me a wink,
I wonder what he could think.
While octopuses play peek-a-boo,
I can't help but join the view!

With sea cucumbers throwing a bash,
My dance moves cause quite a splash.
A clumsy seal joins the crew,
Rolling and tumbling, oh what a zoo!

So here I stand, in fibrous glee,
With little fish contemplating me.
Let the waves tickle my feet,
In this green world, life feels complete!

Depths of Blue

Where fishies wear glasses, oh what a sight,
And jellyfish jiggle, what a funny plight.
A crab with a sandwich, he's quite the chef,
Just pinching his bread, no worries, no stress.

The seagulls all gossip, sharing their lore,
While dolphins play hopscotch, what a beachy chore.
A starfish in slippers, prancing with flair,
In the dance of the tides, he wiggles without care.

The waves are all laughing, what a jolly crew,
As swimmers go splashing, in humor so blue.
With splashy computations, they make quite a mess,
In the depths of delight, no sign of distress.

A whale tells a joke, with a splash and a grin,
While octopuses cheer, waving all of their fin.
In the depths of the blue, where laughter prevails,
Even the crabs can't resist cracking jokes and tales.

Heights of Green

In a jungle of laughter, the monkeys all swing,
With laughter so loud, oh the joy that they bring.
A parrot's on karaoke, belting out tunes,
While sloths groove slowly beneath leafy monsoons.

A lizard in sunglasses, sunbathing with grace,
Sipping on smoothies, what a tropical space!
As turtles in tutus dance under tall trees,
A conga line formed, in the warm summer breeze.

The vines whisper secrets, in chuckles and cheer,
While frogs do the foxtrot, celebrating the year.
With colors so vivid, a bright, leafy scheme,
In heights of the greens, it's the land of a dream.

From roots to the leaves, there's fun all around,
With nature as the stage, joyfully profound.
In a world full of giggles, oh, let's not be shy,
On the heights of the green, every laugh aims to fly.

Horizon's Edge where Waves Meet Leaves

At the horizon's edge, where the waves gently crash,
The trees play a game, tossing coconuts like cash.
A fish on a surfboard, riding high on a swell,
While a crab shimmies, casting its shell spell.

Palm trees are clapping, their fronds in a dance,
With sand as their stage, they take every chance.
A pelican's punning, with humor so vast,
As sea turtles cheer, they're having a blast.

Seashells are giggling, they chatter with joy,
While starfish set up, a beachside decoy.
The laughter is bouncing, from leaf to the foam,
At the horizon's edge, they all feel at home.

As the sun sets in hues, of orange and pink,
Everyone's laughing, their worries in the sink.
In this funny fusion, of land and of sea,
At the horizon's edge, it's pure jubilee!

Sunlit Waters and Tropical Visions

In sunlit reflections, the fish wear a grin,
Like tiny comedians, they're ready to spin.
A mermaid is juggling, oh look at her flair,
With seashells and seaweed, floating in the air.

Tropical visions float by on a breeze,
While parrots tell stories, putting minds at ease.
A walrus in shades is lounging with style,
Winking at dolphins, they're loving this while.

Coconuts giggle, as they sway on their trees,
While seabirds do pratfalls, with grace and with ease.
In the waters so bright, where the sun likes to play,
Fun reigns supreme, in a playful ballet.

With laughter abounding, and joy in each flick,
They sway to the rhythm, a magical trick.
In sunlit waters, there's a spell on the flow,
Where every wave dances, and happiness grows.

Coral Reflections in Lush Surround

In coral gardens, colors splash and collide,
Where sea urchins chuckle, taking a ride.
Anemones giggle, tickling fish that swim by,
While clownfish are playing, oh me, oh my!

A turtle named Tim, with a humorous hat,
Sails on a bubble, can you imagine that?
With seaweed confetti, they're ready to cheer,
For deep-sea delights that bring laughter near.

The coral's a stage, where creatures perform,
With sea snakes doing splits, they break every norm.
As the fairy wrasse twirls, in a circular leap,
In this sea of mirth, they take a joyful sweep.

In lush underwater, where surprises abound,
Every splash sparkles, in laughter they're drowned.
So come dive in deep, where fun takes its stand,
In coral reflections, joy spreads through the sand.

A Haven Where Blue Meets Green

In this land of sea and trees,
Where seagulls dance with the breeze,
A crab in a shell wears a hat,
Sipping from a coconut, how about that?

The waves burp and bubble, oh so sly,
While fish below just roll their eyes,
A flip-flop thief steals a flip, with glee,
As I chase him down, my drink spills on me.

Palm trees wave like they're in a race,
With coconuts bouncing, oh what a chase!
The sun winks down with a playful grin,
Saying, "Join the fun, let the frolic begin!"

So here we laugh, in the salty air,
In a paradise funny, no room for despair,
With each splash, we find delight,
In this haven where colors unite!

Enchanted Mornings by the Coast

Morning breaks with a pelican's dive,
Trying to win the breakfast prize,
The toast keeps floating, and I just stare,
As jellyfish giggle without a care.

A conch shell tells stories like a nosey friend,
As I sip my drink that seems to never end,
With sunglasses on, I squint at the shore,
And wonder how many drinks there's in store?

The sun plays peekaboo behind each cloud,
While beachgoers giggle, getting loud,
Straw hats fly like they're on a spree,
Caught by a breeze, now look at me!

We dance on sand, our troubles build high,
But with every step, they just pass by,
The morning is magic, full of surprise,
In the laughter that twinkles in our eyes!

Tempest and Tranquility

A storm rolls in, with a playful sneer,
Blowing away all my chips and beer,
The sky frowns, while I hold on tight,
To my rainbow umbrella that's lost the fight.

The wind howls like a banshee at play,
While I slip on seashells, oh what a day!
A wave crashes down, I'm soaked to the bone,
And I can't help laughing, all alone.

Then calm sets in, with a wink from the sun,
I shake off the water, the fun's just begun,
Seagulls rearrange the sand on my seat,
As if to say, "Welcome back, have a treat!"

So cheers to the chaos, the splash and the spin,
In this dance with the elements, we all just grin,
With storm clouds and sunshine, we find our cheer,
In a world that's wacky, but oh so dear!

Dancing with Siren's Bounty

The sirens sing in a playful tune,
While I chase fish under the luminous moon,
They wink and giggle as I do the twist,
With sand in my shoes, oh how could I resist?

Starfish are judges for our sandy dance,
With doodle-bugs joining, it's quite the romance,
A dolphin belly flops, aiming for a score,
While I trip on a wave and tumble ashore.

Coconuts cheer with a rhythm so sweet,
As I do cartwheels, feeling the beat,
The merman laughs while the seaweed sways,
In this watery revelry, we spend our days.

So let's toast to laughter, to joy on the tide,
With sirens and shells dancing by our side,
As we whirl in the bright, breezy sea-foam,
In our funny little paradise, we feel right at home!

www.ingramcontent.com/pod-product-compliance
Lightning Source LLC
Chambersburg PA
CBHW072129070526
44585CB00016B/1592